## TRANSCRIBED by JOHN ROBERT BROWN

All of the chord symbols shown are at concert pitch, a minor third higher than the Eb saxophone part.

One of the delightful aspects of the alto saxophone is the way that great jazz players have projected their own unmistakable styles through the instrument. From the cool of Lee Konitz and Paul Desmond to the heat of Charlie Parker, from the intensity of Eric Dolphy to the driving swing of Richie Cole and Phil Woods, the alto saxophone has the chameleon-like ability to adapt to these various styles. Of the twenty titles in Jazz Sax 2, eighteen are transcriptions of recorded performances by some of the greatest altoists in jazz history. The other two transcriptions have been adapted for the alto from performances on closely related members of the saxophone family — Frank Trumbauer's famous C melody saxophone solo on Singin' The Blues, and Roland Kirk's performance of Skater's Waltz, recorded on the stritch, a 'straightened out' version of the alto.

Saxophonist and arranger John Robert Brown is a Senior Lecturer on the full-time staff at the City of Leeds College of Music, where he has taught harmony and directed ensembles on the Jazz and Light Music course since 1975. He is a Vice-President of the Clarinet and Saxophone Society of Great Britain. His other IMP publications include Jazz Trumpet, Jazz Sax, and Jazz Clarinet books 1 and 2.

First Published 1986
© International Music Publications

Exclusive Distributors
International Music Publications
Southend Road, Woodford Green,
Essex IG8 8HN, England.

215-2-390

# Foreword

JULIAN 'CANNONBALL' ADDERLEY enjoyed instant stardom in a way rarely encountered in jazz. In the summer of 1955 Adderley was a 26 year old high school teacher in Fort Lauderdale. On a visit to New York he asked to sit in with Oscar Pettiford's group at the Cafe Bohemia — and brought the house down. Within a few days he made his debut LP, and a very successful jazz career was under way. He played with a rich polished tone, warm vibrato, and a feeling for bounced quavers reminiscent of Benny Carter's style. A FOGGY DAY was issued in Britain in 1964 on Fontana FJL 107 (683 257). Cannonball Adderley died in 1975.

Widely recognised as one of the great post-Charlie Parker alto saxophonists, PHIL WOODS won the Down Beat 'New Star' award in 1956, and has been winning jazz polls ever since. In the late 1970s he was heard by a wider audience as the saxophonist on the Billy Joel hit 'Just The Way You Are', and has also worked on many occasions with film composer Michel Legrand. Characteristics of his playing are polished sound and intonation, combined with fluency and considerable heat and energy. Favourite devices are growls, varied density honking on repeated notes, and wide vibrato on a choked note. He has influenced a whole generation of younger players, most notably Richie Cole. Issued on the double album 'THE PHIL WOODS SIX — LIVE FROM THE SHOWBOAT', (number RCS PL 02202(2)), A SLEEPIN' BEE was recorded in November 1976.

'I'm sure if you've heard of the saxophone you've heard of JOHNNY HODGES' was how Duke Ellington introduced his great alto soloist to an enthusiastic Newport Festival audience in 1956. Hodges (born 1906) was with Ellington for 41 years, and became one of the most important jazz alto saxophonists, equalled or surpassed only by Benny Carter and Charlie Parker. His 'bedroom alto' style of romantic playing, with poised tone and wide scoops and glissandi, was instantly recognisable, and provided a generation of Hollywood composers with the prototype of a great mood-setting sound for romantic scenes. ANITRA'S DANCE is an example of the up-tempo side of his playing. It appears on 'DUKE ELLINGTON AND HIS ORCHESTRA' re-issued in 1980 on CBS Classics, number 61899.

The characteristics of the 'West Coast' style of jazz are epitomised in the playing and writing of LENNIE NIEHAUS, though BLUE ROOM is somewhat unusual in that the improvisations are played over a harmonic progression that differs considerably from that used for the melody statement. This performance was recorded in January and February 1955, and issued under the title 'LENNIE NIEHAUS VOL. 3: THE OCTET, NO. 2.' The original number was Contemporary LAC 12054, but the record was reissued in 1986 with the same title, but re-numbered Contemporary COP 107.

If Lennie Niehaus epitomises the West Coast style then surely PAUL DESMOND is the epitome of the Cool era. Paul once named Pete Brown and Lee Konitz as his influences; CAMPTOWN RACES is pure Desmond. His solo is notable not only because it successfully meets the challenge of playing on one chord, but because the saxophonist builds the improvisation from the notes of a pentatonic scale, an appropriate choice to match the folksy mood of the Stephen Foster song. The solo first appeared on Dave Brubeck's 'Southern Scene' album, but was reissued on 'DAVE BRUBECK'S GREATEST HITS' on CBS 32046.

BENNY CARTER was born in 1907. By the early 1930s he had worked with Duke Ellington and Fletcher Henderson, and in 1933 worked in England as the staff arranger for Henry Hall. CRAZY RHYTHM appears on what is probably his best-known album, 'Further Definitions'. This was recorded in 1961 and issued on Impulse, number AS 12 (801608).

'The living university of jazz' is how one jazz critic described Art Blakey's Jazz Messengers, and it's true that a list of musicians employed by Blakey during his long career makes impressive reading. The early 1980's was a particularly strong time for the Messengers, with band members including the Marsalis brothers, Terence Blanchard and altoist BOBBY WATSON. His solo on FALLING IN LOVE WITH LOVE appears on 'Straight Ahead', on Concord CJ 168, issued in 1981.

LEE KONITZ was at the heart of the jazz avant-garde from the very beginning of his career. A member of the influential 'Birth-of-the-Cool' band under Miles Davis' leadership in 1948, he was also closely associated with the experiments of pianist Lennie Tristano. Konitz has a cool thin sound, with little vibrato, and employs an oblique approach to melody. This is typified by his theme statement in I REMEMBER YOU which, whilst retaining composer Victor Schertzinger's notes, redistributes them with little care for the opinions of those who like to recognise the tune. Recorded in 1961, this performance appears on 'Motion', on Verve 821 553-1.

ARTHUR BLYTHE has been consistently placed in the top half-dozen in the alto sax category in American jazz polls in recent years. JUST A CLOSER WALK WITH THEE appears on the 1981 record 'Blythe Spirit', on CBS 85194.

JAMES OSTEND 'PETE' BROWN was born in 1906. He gained his reputation with Frankie Newton and John Kirby groups of the early 1930's, but his name is well-known in today's jazz circles because of his frequently-cited influence on Paul Desmond. OH, LADY, BE GOOD was recorded in 1961, two years before Brown's death, and issued on 77 Records, number 77LA 12/8.

ON THE SUNNY SIDE OF THE STREET was recorded by TAB SMITH when he was a member of a band led by Coleman Hawkins, 'Coleman Hawkins And His Sax Ensemble', in May 1944. It was issued on Mercury MMB 12013 and reissued on Fontana FJL 131.

Charlie Parker's influence on young saxophonists was tremendous, and there is a whole group of important players born in the late twenties and early thirties who took up Bird's way of playing. These included Leo Wright, Jackie McLean, Gigi Gryce, Sonny Criss, Hank Crawford — and LOU DONALDSON. O SOLE MIO was recorded in New York on June 19th 1964 and issued on Argo TL 1152.

Although he came to prominence during his stay with the Stan Kenton band between 1947 and 1952, ART PEPPER is today remembered more for his biography 'Straight Life' (a tale of narcotics, ill health and prison interspersed with music) and for a handful of memorable later albums. It's from one of these, 'Modern Jazz Classics' (Contemporary LAC 12229), which uses an eleven piece band and Marty Paich's arrangements, that this 1959 version of 'ROUND MIDNIGHT is taken.

No apologies are offered for including in this collection a solo that was not originally conceived on the alto saxophone. The C Melody saxophone is nowadays rarely used, but its light delicate sound was the perfect expressive medium for FRANKIE TRUMBAUER, and luckily his outstanding solo on SINGIN' THE BLUES fits perfectly into the alto range and key without any change in pitch. This solo was recorded on February 4th 1927 in the company of Bix Beiderbecke. It was a commercial success at the time, and has been justly celebrated ever since, enjoying countless reissues.

The late SONNY STITT recorded his magnificent version of Hoagy Carmichael's STARDUST in 1955, in an arrangement by Quincy Jones. It was released on Vogue, number LAE 12171.

The word 'incredible' crops up whenever the life and career of ROLAND KIRK is discussed. Blind from the age of two, he was blessed with massive energy and inventiveness. He pioneered the art of playing three saxophones simultaneously, was one of the first jazz reed players to employ circular breathing, and demonstrated the possibilities of humming along with his own flute playing in a two-part texture. He also played some unusual variants of the saxophone family, particularly the manzello (a variant of the soprano saxophone) and the stritch — a straightened-out alto saxophone which goes straight down to the floor. The stritch is used for SKATER'S WALTZ. It was recorded on July 11th 1961, and reissued in 1978 on Prestige PR 24080.

CHARLIE PARKER stands at the centre of post-war jazz alto saxophone, and many would hold him to be the greatest soloist in jazz, regardless of instrument. THE SONG IS YOU (take 3) was recorded on December 30th 1952, WHY DO I LOVE YOU (take 2) on March 12th 1951. Both have been repeatedly reissued.

Yet another short-lived musician (he died just after his 36th birthday) ERIC DOLPHY bridges the gap between Bebop and the innovations of the avant-garde. THEY ALL LAUGHED was recorded on June 26th 1960. It was first released in 1960 on the album 'Looking Ahead', and reissued in 1978 on 'Fire Waltz', number Prestige PR 24085.

Born in 1948, RICHIE COLE started playing the alto saxophone in junior school, having his first lessons at the age of 10 and studying with Phil Woods from the age of 15. Woods' influence is still noticeable. In 1983 Richie Cole collected 18,000 votes from readers of Japan's Swing Journal, voting him number one alto player. In fact, WILLOW WEEP FOR ME was recorded in Japan. It was issued in Europe on the album 'Cool 'C'', on Muse MR 5245.

# The Blue Room

Saxophone Solo by LENNIE NIEHAUS

Words by LORENZ HART
Music by RICHARD RODGERS

7

# Camptown Races

Saxophone Solo by PAUL DESMOND

STEPHEN FOSTER

# Anitra's Dance

Saxophone Solo by JOHNNY HODGES

GRIEG

# Crazy Rhythm

Saxophone Solo by BENNY CARTER

Words by IRVING CAESAR
Music by JOSEPH MEYER and ROGER WOLFEKAHN

# Falling In Love With Love

Saxophone Solo by BOBBY WATSON

Words by LORENZ HART
Music by RICHARD RODGERS

♩ = 184

# A Foggy Day

Saxophone Solo by CANNONBALL ADDERLEY

Words by IRA GERSHWIN
Music by GEORGE GERSHWIN

# I Remember You

Saxophone Solo by LEE KONITZ

Words by JOHNNY MERCER
Music by VICTOR SCHERTZINGER

# Oh, Lady, Be Good!

Saxophone Solo by PETE BROWN

Words by IRA GERSHWIN
Music by GEORGE GERSHWIN

# O Sole Mio

Saxophone Solo by LOU DONALDSON

TRADITIONAL

Rubato - Slowly

In tempo
♩ = 138

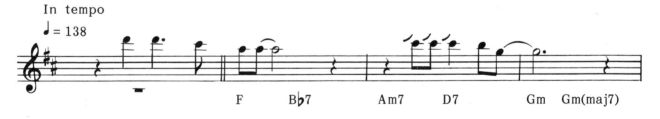

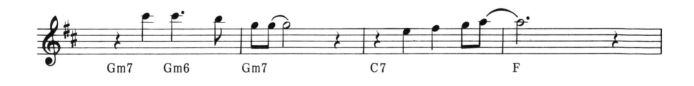

# Just A Closer Walk With Thee

Saxophone Solo by ARTHUR BLYTHE

TRADITIONAL

# On The Sunny Side Of The Street

Saxophone Solo by TAB SMITH

Words by DOROTHY FIELDS
Music by JIMMY McHUGH

# 'Round Midnight

Saxophone Solo by ART PEPPER

Words by BERNIE HANIGHEN
Music by COOTIE WILLIAMS and THELONIOUS MONK

31

32

# Singin' The Blues

Saxophone Solo by FRANK TRUMBAUER

Words by SAM LEWIS and JOE YOUNG
Music by CON CONRAD and J RUSSEL ROBINSON

# The Skater's Waltz

Saxophone Solo by ROLAND KIRK

WALDTEUFEL

# A Sleepin' Bee

Saxophone Solo by PHIL WOODS

Words by TRUMAN CAPOTE and HAROLD ARLEN
Music by HAROLD ARLEN

40

42

# The Song Is You

*Saxophone Solo by CHARLIE PARKER*

Words by OSCAR HAMMERSTEIN II
Music by JEROME KERN

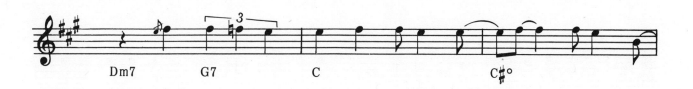

# They All Laughed

Saxophone Solo by ERIC DOLPHY

Words by IRA GERSHWIN
Music by GEORGE GERSHWIN

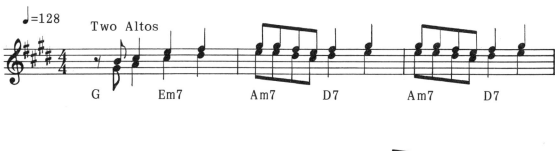

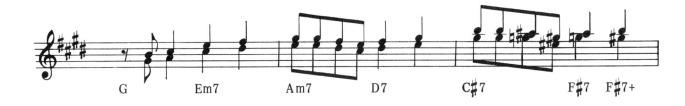

A7            Am7        D7

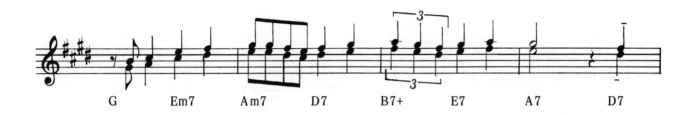

G    Em7    Am7    D7    B7+    E7    A7    D7

G    Em7    Am7    D7    G       Into Solos

Dolphy's solo

G    Em7    Am7    D7

Am7    D7    G    D7

G    Em7    Am7    D7

G                                    D7

G              Em7              Am7          D7

C#7          F#7      F#7+      Bm7          E7

Em7                              A7

Am7                        D7

G                        G7          E7

# Stardust

Saxophone Solo by SONNY STITT

Words by MITCHELL PARISH
Music by HOAGY CARMICHAEL

54

# Why Do I Love You?

Saxophone Solo by CHARLIE PARKER

Words by OSCAR HAMMERSTEIN II
Music by JEROME KERN

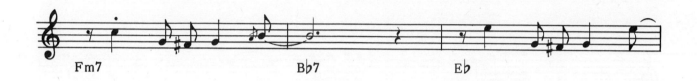

# Willow Weep For Me

Saxophone Solo by RICHIE COLE

Words and Music
by ANN RONNELL

Rubato - Slowly

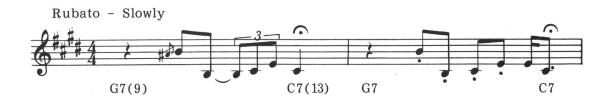

In tempo, 12 in a bar feel
♩ = 60

60

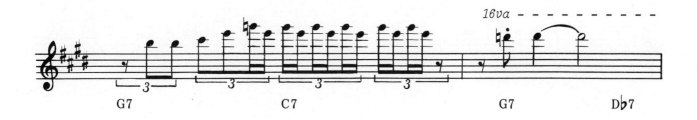

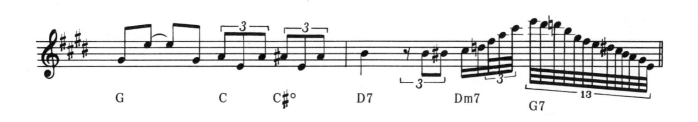

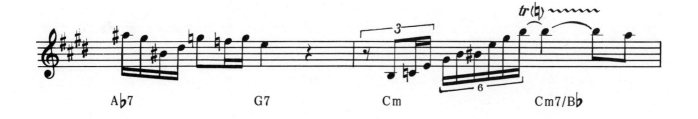

62

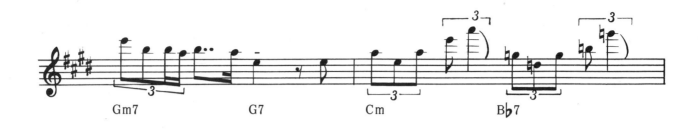

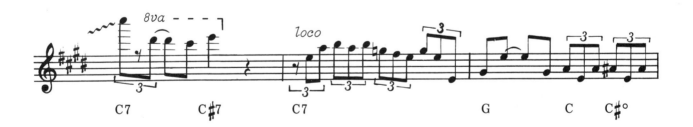

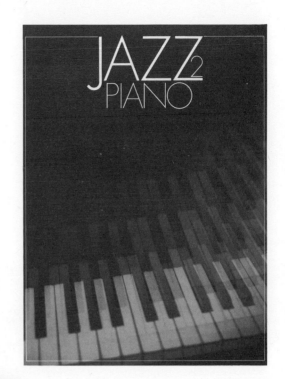

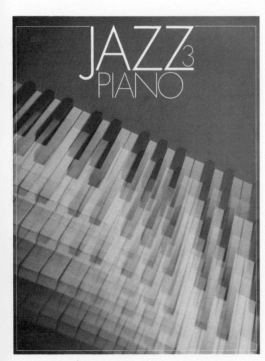

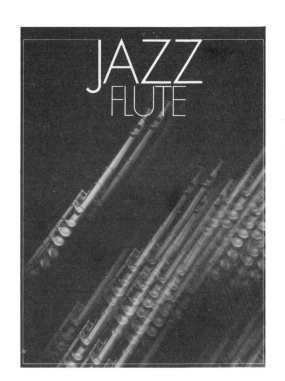

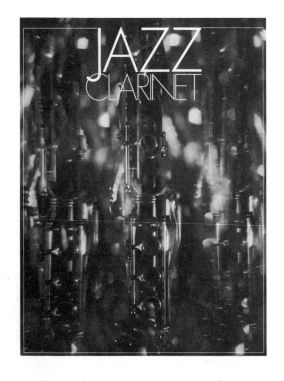